CAMOUFLAGE
& COLOUR

CAMOUFLAGE & COLOUR

LIZ BOMFORD

Photographs from the Bruce Coleman
Wildlife & Travel Photo Collection

BOXTREE

First published 1992 by
Boxtree Limited
36 Tavistock Street
London WC2E 7PB

Text © Liz Bomford

Edited by Miranda Smith
Designed by Sarah Hall

Colour reproduction by Fotographics Limited, Hong Kong
Typeset by Cambrian Typesetters, Frimley, Surrey
Printed and bound by Dai Nippon, Hong Kong

A CIP catalogue record for this book is available from the British Library

ISBN 1–85283–170–7

ACKNOWLEDGEMENTS

All pictures courtesy of Bruce Coleman Wildlife & Travel Photo Collection:
Erwin and Peggy Bauer 80; Jane Burton 40, 52, 55, 63, 68, 70, 74, 88, 97,
103, 108, 113; Bob and Clara Calhoun 39, 123; Brian J. Coates 38 above, 82,
83, 119; Bruce Coleman 87; Alain Compost 75; Gerald Cubitt 47; Peter
Davey 81; A. J. Deane 46; Halle Flygare 66; M. P. L. Fogden 3, 58, 62, 109,
120, 126, 127; Jeff Foott Productions 8, 122; Neville Fox-Davies 104; C. B.
and D. W. Frith 59; Frithfoto 44; Frances Furlong 42; Dennis Green 54; M. P.
Kahl 65; Stephen J. Krasemann 118; Felix Labhardt 121; Gordon Langsbury
67, 94; Frans Lanting 4, 38 below, 85 below; John Markham 96; George
McCarthy 78, 101; Dr S. Nielsen 50, 51, 76, 98, 99; Charlie Ott 56; Dieter
Plage 79; Dieter and Mary Plage 115; Dr Eckart Pott 57; M. P. Price 41; Andy
Purcell 24, 107, 116; Hans Reinhard 13, 16, 61, 100, 102; Carl Roessler 73;
Norbert Rosing 60; Leonard Lee Rue 10, 28, 84; Gary Rutherford 106; Dr
Friedrich Sauer 69, 92, 114; Kim Taylor 21, 26, 43, 45, 71, 90, 124, 125;
Wolfgang Trolenberg 85 above; Jan van de Kam 95; Peter Ward 110, 111,
112; Rod Williams 48, 49; Bill Wood 72, 117; Konrad Wothe 91; Jonathan
T. Wright 36; Gunther Ziesler 30, 35, 86, 89; J. Zwaenepoel 64

CONTENTS

FOREWORD

Glancing around nervously, we slithered down the bank and stepped with care over the jetsom lining the river's edge. This, we were assured by our guide, was the very spot where all the crocodiles came to breed. In fact, we were standing right in the middle of it! As a couple of reptilian eyes rose out of the murky water close by, I was suddenly uncomfortably aware of my inability to distinguish between mud and animal between the cracked surface of the rotting bark that lay all around and living skin.

Out of touch with the life and death struggles of the wild, humans seldom experience the acute awareness of the natural environment that must be the inheritance of all wild creatures. I do not believe they live in fear, but rather that both predator and prey exist in a state of stress, using wits sharpened one against the other. Twenty thousand years ago, hunter-gatherers learned through dance and ritual to align their souls with those of wild animals, to recognize them in their many disguises. These things no longer concern us. The price of civilization, it seems, is a kind of blindness, vision is largely a mental process and urban people pay attention to different stimuli as they cross roads, catch buses and watch television.

Have we entirely lost touch with the wild? Fortunately for humankind, the ancient arts of birdwatching, mammal-tracking and hunting still flourish. Cracking the camouflage, honing recognition to a split second, these are skills as old as our species. We are no longer in danger from predators, but never before has there been such an urgent need to remain alert to the state of the environment. The consequences of our blindness lie all around us. We ignore the death-throes of the natural world at our peril.

LIZ BOMFORD

INTRODUCTION

We are surrounded by colour. It is so much part of our lives that we take it for granted. Our eyes automatically adjust to it. Our brains, so busy with other things, only occasionally register its hues. If we think about it at all, it is perhaps only because we have noticed something unusual. Colour is what gives our world beauty, but the appreciation – the perception – of colour is not the work of the eye but of the mind.

It is easy to assume that the natural world has acquired its colours as a happy accident. Nothing could be further from the truth. Every species on the face of the earth has evolved a strategy for survival, and colour is a vital part of that strategy. The evolution of each creature's colour has occurred over millions of years, alongside the development of form and behaviour.

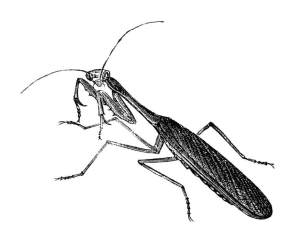

CAMOUFLAGE AND COLOUR

Underpinning the survival games that animals play is a physical world of minerals and plants, where the exhibition of colour seems arbitrary. Does it benefit a ruby to be red? The answer is no – it is the chemical structure that determines the colour. In the living world, there is an element of flexibility. Plants must be green because they eat with their leaves, and chlorophyll (which is a green pigment) is essential to photosynthesis. But plants are living things and have evolved colour strategies in a complex display of flowers aimed at the insect world, in the interest of sexual reproduction.

One of the most widespread uses of colour is for hiding and disguise. Predators as well as prey may enter into a 'colour war' with each other, where the ability to use cryptic coloration to melt into the landscape assumes life or death importance.

Colour stimulates the brain and provokes an emotional response in humans. Our spirits lift in bright sunshine when colours are reflected brilliantly, and we feel out of sorts when the sky is overcast for long periods. Although it is dangerous to make assumptions about what animals feel, it is likely that they too experience strong emotions in response to certain colours. Birds and fish adopt brighter breeding plumage and brilliant scales to trigger sexual excitement. Equally, colour displays can stimulate fear and warn intruders to keep away. A brightly coloured animal is likely to be using colour as a tool to get a particular response.

WHAT IS COLOUR?

White light is made up of the spectral colours of red, orange, yellow, green, blue, indigo and violet. You can discover these in the refractive action of a crystal, or split by droplets of moisture and painted across the sky in a rainbow.

The colours represent different wavelengths of light. When white light falls on a coloured object some wavelengths are absorbed and some reflected. When we look at that object we see the reflected light which is a mixture of the rejected colour wavelengths.

When an object absorbs the full spectrum of light falling on it, we see it as black. When all the wavelengths are reflected, we see the object as white.

HOW IS COLOUR MADE?

There are two ways in which objects determine their own colour. Chemical compounds called pigments selectively absorb and reflect particular wavelengths of light. However, there are also structural colours which are created by the physical nature of the object. Some colours are caused by a combination of the two methods.

The pigment melanin is manufactured by animals themselves, often from the waste products of their digestion. It is laid down in droplets or granules within the structure of fur, feathers, scales and skin. Melanin pigments are the cause of black, brown, dull red and some of the yellows. It is melanin that colours human hair and gives baby chicks their yellow feathers.

Carotenoid pigments give rise to bright orange, red and yellow. Plants like carrots are full of it. Animals cannot make carotenoids, they must get them by eating plants or herbivores that have themselves been eating plants containing the pigments. Carotenoids can be modified to create other colours. Lobsters are a vivid indigo blue when they are alive. This is caused by a carotenoid pigment allied with a protein. When the lobster is cooked, the protein breaks down, leaving the carotenoid intact, and the body of the lobster pink.

There is a third group of pigments called pterins. They occur largely in the insect world and are made from the waste products of the body's metabolism.

Some of the duller blues and greens are derived from pigments similar to chlorophyll which gives colour to leaves. Although animals often obtain the pigments that determine their colour through food, they seem unable to make use of chlorophyll at all. As a result, green is an unusual colour in the animal kingdom. Even the colours of green caterpillars are obtained from the mixing of yellow and blue pigments rather than from the plants on which they feed.

OPPOSITE PAGE
Albinos, like this donkey and her foal, are born with no melanin pigment in their bodies. They are frequently outcasts among their own kind because their snowy coats make them conspicuous. Their vision is poor due to lack of melanin and they do not survive long in the wild as their colour makes them natural targets for predators.

STRUCTURAL COLOURS

White and the brightest shades of blue and green are structural colours caused by the scattering of light by tiny particles. The best example of this is the sky. The blue of the heavens is created when short wavelengths of sunlight reflected by the earth are scattered and reflected back to earth again by dust particles in the atmosphere. Seen against the black background of space, the effect is brilliant blue.

Called Tyndall scattering, this structural colour is the cause of blue eyes in humans, as well as the blue feathers of many birds such as parrots, toucans, kingfishers, and the stunning Blue bird-of-paradise. The creation of blue by Tyndall scattering depends on two things, a light scattering layer and a black background.

Babies are born with blue eyes. This is because minute protein particles in the iris scatter short wavelengths of light which are seen against a black melanin layer at the back of the iris. As time goes by, some children develop brown eyes as brown melanin pigment develops in the iris to mask the effect of the scattering particles. Albinos are totally lacking in melanin pigment. Their eyes look pink because the iris has no dark melanin to create a black background. As a result, the blood capillaries at the back of the eye dominate the blue effect of Tyndall scattering.

Pigmentary colours and structural colours sometimes influence each other in delightful ways. The brilliant green of certain parrots, chameleons, frogs, snakes and lizards is created when light passes through a yellow filter before hitting the blue Tyndall scattering layer. The light is then reflected back once more through the yellow filter to create a really strong effect.

Keen budgie breeders manipulate the genes of wild green budgerigars to create different colours: birds bred with no yellow pigment are blue, budgies with no black pigment are yellow, and budgies bred with no pigment at all are white.

INTERFERENCE COLOURS

Take a closer look at the crow's wing or the back of a starling. Although the bird is basically black or brown, there is a sheen to the feathers and in sunlight they are positively iridescent. The colours shimmer as the bird moves and the effect varies according to your angle of view. The head of a drake mallard can change from green to purple and back again in front of your eyes. What causes this?

Animals in peak condition build up extra keratin on their coats. The keratin allows most of the light that falls upon it to pass through, reach the pigment and be reflected outwards once more. Some light, however, just bounces off the surface of the keratin itself. The result is that there are two different wavelengths vibrating in opposite directions alongside each other. So, although the animal may be a dull colour normally, in bright sunlight, it can take on 'false' hues.

The iridescent effect is used by brightly-coloured animals as well. Although pheasants are hard to spot when skulking in the undergrowth, their feathers are rich in colour which shimmers gloriously in sunlight when 'false' iridescent colours are added. Hummingbirds and sunbirds as well as many butterflies and insects use the tropical sun to enhance already brilliant colours.

In the gloom of the sea it is hard to see colours. Even divers have difficulty because the longer wavelengths of light cannot penetrate far into the water. Shades of red are only visible in the shallows. At fifteen metres, eveything looks greeny-blue and even the most vividly coloured fish seems dull. Interference

colours are often used to enhance the colours of fish that live amongst the shadows of caves or rocky overhangs. These colours are particularly effective, created as they are by a partially reflective layer on the surface of the fishes' scales interfering with the reflected wavelength. Animals that live in dark environments use eye-catching colour for communication. One problem with interference colours is that they cannot be switched off. The way to become inconspicuous is to hide, which may be the reason the brightest coloured fish are usually found in a rocky or coral environment.

Cuttlefish enhance their extensive array of pigment colours with iridescence. However, ctenophores, or comb jellies, achieve their colours by a different method. Glands provide luminescence and the flashing light is diffracted around the edge of a ctenophore's body. Another form of interference, diffraction, splits the wavelengths into bands that break up the light into different colours.

BIOLUMINESCENCE

While most plants and animals use sunlight to create colour, some manufacture their own light. In the deep sea, around 1,500 species of fish have turned biochemist and create light where otherwise there would be none. Bioluminescence is the result of the chemical reaction of a substance – generally luciferin – with an enzyme called a luciferase. Under the control of the organism that carries them, the two are brought together to produce light for a variety of purposes.

There are two kinds of bioluminescence. Some creatures, such as the viperfish, have luminous photophores. Arranged in rows along the body, these structures have complex lenses, reflectors and pigmented screens. Light is produced by photogenic cells and reflected out through a lens and cornea-like skin. The second way of obtaining bioluminescent light is to act as host for luminous bacteria. The bacteria are nurtured in special organs, so they stay in peak condition and produce the maximum amount of light. In some species there are structural devices like shutters to enable the fish to turn out the light when it is not required.

Surprisingly, fish do not need light in deep water so much to see by as to hide behind. Light can be used as camouflage. Silhouetted against the light trickling down from the surface, midwater fish are vulnerable to predators that lurk beneath them. This is why so many fish only feed at night. However, even soft moonlight can be a problem. The strategy of fish like the California midshipman is to produce a weak glow from the luminous photophores on its belly to counter the silhouette effect of moonlight. Diurnal fish mimic the wavelength and intensity of sunlight filtering down from the surface to make themselves invisible. Ctenophores also use bioluminescence to defend themselves. When touched they emit a burst of light that may dazzle or confuse the predator.

The most intense light is found in several species of anomalopid Flashlight fish. They use bioluminescent light as we would use a torch to search out their prey. The light organ is situated below the eye, and it can emit a beam powerful enough to be seen up to thirty metres away. The light flashes on and off as the Flashlight fish blinks or rotates the light organ inside a dark pocket.

In the absence of sunlight, no plants exist to create carbohydrates through photosynthesis. At the bottom of the food chain, the small fish of the deep depend on detritus falling from the upper, sunlit levels of the sea for food. There is never enough, and all deep-sea fish must conserve energy. Instead of chasing prey, angler fish use a bioluminescent fishing pole, which is a modified dorsal spine, to entice small fish to swim near its mouth.

Bioluminescence can be disconcerting when encountered on land. When camping alone in the heart of a tropical forest on the island of Nosy Mangabe, Madagascar, I woke in the middle of the night to discover my tent surrounded by a carpet of green bioluminescence. I ran the glowing soil through my fingers, realizing that the effect was caused by microscopic fungi. An hour or so later, it was gone, and in the morning there was no trace of it.

Although bioluminescence is rare on land, fireflies have luminescent organs on their abdomens that emit an extremely bright light to attract the opposite sex. They are common beetles in warm countries, but there are 1,300 different species. The subtle differences in bioluminescent signal help them to identify appropriate sexual partners. Some fireflies do not fly as adults and are commonly called glow-worms.

SLOW COLOUR CHANGE

The colours of most animals are fixed for long periods of time, but there are seasonal opportunities to change coat. Birds are obliged to moult their feathers at least once a year

because they wear out. This offers an opportunity to change colour either to produce fancy plumage for the breeding season, or warm and cryptic feathers for winter. There is usually one major moult of all feathers and one or two smaller moults of body feathers. Moulting is an energy-draining business which takes a surprisingly long time to complete. Birds cannot fly efficiently with feathers missing so they must finish moulting before they undertake migration.

Some birds shed all their flight feathers at once after breeding and become drab in colour and completely flightless for a few weeks. Waterbirds such as grebes and divers prefer this method because, although it makes them vulnerable to predators, they can always paddle into deeper water if threatened. Eider duck in particular form large unkempt-looking flocks on the surface of the sea at this time of year.

Within a few weeks of hatching, fledglings must moult out of their fluffy nest attire into something more suitable for flight. Baby penguins cannot afford to lose any feathers at all – it is too cold in their environment and they need the insulation. They need cryptic adult coloration to catch fish. To maintain insulation, new feathers simply grow into the old ones. The effect is very ragged, but the birds do not die of exposure and the old feathers are soon preened away from the new plumage.

Another kind of colour change is effected by gradually altering the types and quantities of pigment in the skin. It is not very fast, but it is a flexible process and many animals use it to adjust to seasonal changes.

Crab spiders have to change colour several times during the year because their life-strategy is to lurk inconspicuously inside the flowers of plants that are attractive to insects. In order to catch their prey, they take on the exact colour of the flower. When the flowering season of one species comes to an end, the crab spider must alter colour and take up residence in another. This change takes between five and twenty days. The North American species *Misumena vatia* changes colour from white to yellow when it moves from ox-eye daisies or white fleabane to golden rod in July or August.

Flatfish such as plaice, brill and turbot have two methods of changing colour. The first is a slow one – the gradual reorganization of colour pigments in the skin to enable the fish to blend with either a bright sandy bottom or a dark and muddy substrate. These colour changes are associated with alterations in flatfish behaviour and migration to new habitats as they mature. The second method is similar to that used by chameleons, and involves the manipulation of the colour pigments in the upper layer of the skin to effect an immediate colour change.

FAST COLOUR CHANGE

Those quick change artists, the chameleons, octopus and cuttlefish, have been able to develop speedy colour changing techniques because their bodies are covered in bare skin. Refreshed continuously by blood, their skin is under the direct control of muscle activity. It can be manipulated in ways that fur and feather cannot.

Fast colour-change is effected by specialized cells called chromatophores which lie in a superficial layer of the skin and contain melanin colour pigments. The chromatophore is surrounded by an elastic membrane which is controlled by muscle fibres that radiate outwards. When the muscles contract, the membrane is stretched flat, fully exposing the dark pigment. As the muscle relaxes, the membrane contracts and the pigment granules are pulled together, disappearing from view and allowing lighter pigments lying deeper in the skin to be seen. Most species have chromatophores containing three pigments – usually red, yellow and black. A layer of reflecting cells called 'iridocytes' modifies these pigments and increases the range of colours that the animal can use.

Using chromatophores, octopus and cuttlefish can flush their bodies with waves of strong colour at a speed unsurpassed in the animal kingdom. Stripes and strong patterns break up the outline for camouflage purposes, and delicate shading is produced by partially opening certain chromatophores to create an impression of texture.

The mechanism for creating cryptic colour would be

OPPOSITE PAGE

Pigmentary colours can blend with structural colours. In the feathers of these budgerigars, light passes through a yellow pigment filter before hitting a Tyndall blue scattering layer lying over a dark melanin background. Budgerigar breeders can manipulate the genes of wild green budgerigars to create different colours. Birds bred with no yellow pigment are blue; those with no black pigments turn out yellow, whilst budgies with no pigment at all are white.

useless without a reciprocal one for perceiving the colours of the environment. It has been reported that octupus are colour-blind, but this is quite untrue. Like many molluscs, the octupus' skin is light sensitive. Their eyes see only blue and yellow, but tactile stimuli on the suckers of the arms are able to transmit information about the texture and colour of their environment to the brain. So, even a blind octopus can change colour to blend in with its surroundings.

Octopus and cuttlefish can match any background colour, from black to white, in around two-thirds of a second. By sending waves of colour across their bodies, cuttlefish can even simulate the play of light and shade reflected from the surface of the water.

The ability to change colour quickly is important to reptiles and amphibians because it helps them in thermo-regulation. Indeed, this may have been the original function of melanophores, the repertoire of colours for camouflage and social activity being a later sophistication. Sunbathing is essential to warm the body of a reptile or amphibian into activity early in the morning. They generally go darker during this process as the melanophore cells expand to allow the pigment to absorb infra-red (warm) wavelengths as well as the visible light spectrum.

A large number of reptiles and amphibians, notably the chameleons, can change colour quickly, but none match the speed of the molluscs. They use a slightly different method: although they possess chromatophores, they do not stretch the skin to expose the pigment, but instead run the pigment through branched cells in the chromatophore. When the pigment is 'at rest', concentrated at a single point, the colour in other layers of the skin predominates. Lizards and frogs often have three colour-producing layers. At the bottom lies a layer of chromatophores containing colour in pigment form. The skin above holds tiny scattering particles, so it can produce Tyndall blue. The top layer consists of a superficial covering of oil droplets containing yellow carotenoid pigments. Branches from the chromatophore extend into the other two layers of skin making even more variation of colour possible.

Colour change in chameleons is both rapid and complex. Frogs and toads use the same basic method, but it takes them longer to achieve a satisfactory match with the environment. Flatfish such as sole, turbot and plaice hide out on the seabed imitating not only the colour, and also the texture, of mud, sand and gravel.

COLOUR PERCEPTION

We cannot tell what the subjective experience of colour may be for most animals, but we can be sure that the majority see in colour because of the vast number of behavioural strategies that can be easily observed in the animal kingdom. Colour strategy only works if the animal towards whom it is directed can see it. If predators were insensitive to colour, prey animals would not bother with camouflage.

Whilst the existence of cones in the retina of the eye indicates colour vision, it is hard to determine exactly what an animal sees because much depends on the types of colour receptors that exist on the cones in the retina of the eye. (Rods give black and white vision.) Different combinations of colour receptor create different effects with increased sensitivity to certain wavelengths in the colour spectrum. In addition, oil droplets can act like colour filters over the cones. Although most animals have colour receptors, some may see the world predominantly in reds and oranges, while others are most sensitive to greens and blues.

Light stimulates the eye to send certain electrical impulses to the brain. Animals process that information in different ways. Some colours may have no meaning, so they ignore them. For a long time, it was thought that cats, dogs, cows and horses were colour-blind because behavioural tests showed no reactions to colour. Recent post-mortem examinations show that they do have colour receptors, but it is clear that they do not interpret colours as humans do.

Although humans have very good eyesight, it is by no means the most sophisticated in the animal kingdom. Grey squirrels are able to see colours at dusk, where we only see black and grey. Most birds have better eyesight than people. Owls have colour vision as well as excellent eyesight after dark. Insects' compound eyes give extraordinarily good definition and a wide angle of view. Moreover, insects enjoy colour vision which is sensitive to ultra-violet. Those that visit flowers may be drawn by the ultra-violet 'honey-guide' markings on the petals that are invisible to us. Fruit that looks black to us probably appear bright to an insect or bird.

BIRD VISION

Birds have both monocular vision – in which they are able to use each eye independently – and binocular vision – when they see with both eyes together. When a thrush cocks its head to get a better picture of an earthworm, it is directing the light coming into the eye on to the fovea which is a super-sensitive spot on the retina where large numbers of colour sensitive cones are concentrated. Birds that hunt at high speed, such as raptors, kingfishers, terns and swallows, have a second 'temporal' fovea in the rear part of the retina that provides binocular vision. From its vantage-point, high in the sky, the falcon can scan a huge area of countryside as well as examine interesting objects in close-up.

The excellent colour vision of birds has been the force that has determined the majority of the colours of the natural world. Birds are ubiquitous predators on insects, mammals, fish and indeed, other birds. Many flowers need birds to pollinate them, and a host of plants rely on birds to distribute their seeds. A worldwide survey showed that 80 per cent of plants that need birds to pollinate them displayed red flowers.

The sensitivity of birds to red, yellow and green has dictated that caterpillars, frogs and wasps, whose strategy is to display and advertise their poisonous or distasteful qualities, have evolved bodies that are brightly painted in these colours.

Like amphibians and reptiles, but unlike mammals, birds have coloured droplets of oil in the cone cells of the retina which modify colour reception. The droplets are mostly red, orange-red or yellow – all colours with long wavelengths. It seems that the droplets act as selective filters, removing short wavelengths from the blue end of the spectrum. Plant-eating birds like pigeons end up with enhanced colour sensitivity to red, yellow and green – the pigments found in the green leaves of plants. When green chlorophyll breaks down in autumn, the subsidiary pigments red and yellow can be seen

as leaves turn golden before falling. The pigeon's eyesight is acutely adjusted to identify its food.

Oil droplets in the retinal cones act like a photographic filter to cut through atmospheric haze on misty days. The effect of removing blue from the spectrum is to make the sky appear very dark. This is helpful to seabirds because they depend on each other to find shoals of fish. Against a dark sky, white-bodied birds like gulls, albatrosses, terns and gannets are clearly visible to each other, so when one bird dives on a shoal, the others will soon flock round to feed.

The drawback to all filters, whether they are photographic ones placed on the lens of a camera or oil droplets in the cones of a bird's retina, is that they cut down the amount of light passing through them. So less light falls on the film and less light excites the receptors in a bird's eye. Birds that hunt in conditions of poor light, such as owls and nightjars, cannot afford to lose this sensitivity, so they have very few oil droplets in the cones. Swifts, martins and swallows would find it hard to catch insects on the wing against a dark sky, so they too have few colour filters.

Particles in the atmosphere, such as dust, scatter sunlight and create patterns of polarized light which change throughout the day. If we could see polarized light, we would be able to tell the time and use it for navigation as bees do. The patterns it creates in the sky are particularly useful to birds on migration, enabling them to locate the position of the sun, even when it is out of sight, obscured by the horizon or hidden by heavy cloud. Like insects, birds are sensitive to ultra-violet light, another useful aid to navigation.

COLOUR CHANGE WITH AGE

Human beings retain the same shape and colour throughout their lives. We grow considerably bigger as we mature, developing sexually, emotionally and intellectually. However, there are no radical changes to the body, although unfortunately, our colours tend to fade as we get older. Humans are unusual in the animal world. Most animals change their colours to suit their activities at each stage in their lives. As juveniles, they generally need to blend with the environment.

Young deer have spotted coats, useful in the first days after birth when fawns are left alone in the shelter of the undergrowth while the doe feeds. When danger threatens, the fawns instinctively remain quiet and immobile, because they would be easy prey if they tried to run away. The fawns' dappled coats are useful camouflage, but as soon as they are grown and able to run, the spots disappear.

Red fox cubs are born with dark chocolate-coloured fur, as though to blend with the darkness of their natal earth. By the time they emerge to play at the opening of the den, their coats have lightened to a mid-brown colour. As they grow stronger, the vixen takes them on short trips. Like the fawns, young fox cubs will freeze if danger threatens, so the coat needs to be cryptically coloured at first. As summer progresses and the fox cubs get more confident, the coat begins to acquire the rich colours of adulthood. The fox cubs' tails become bushy and their heads become elongated as the adult fox mask appears. Now concealment is not the issue, for the family has grown bold and fleet of foot.

The blatant red coat of the British Red fox signals strength, vitality and approaching sexual maturity. The Red fox's European and American cousins never develop the same bright hue, but perhaps they need to keep cryptic coloration as adults to defend themselves against predators such as wolves and wolverines, which do not exist in Britain.

The chicks of ground-nesting birds face special dangers. Birds that hatch in a cosy nest high in a tree can afford to emerge from the shell naked and helpless. But gulls and terns, partridges and pheasants, grebes and most wading birds must hatch with feathers that will match their surroundings. The eggs and chicks of the Golden plover are almost indistinguishable from the pebbles of the bank on which they are raised.

Whilst the nestlings of the Oystercatcher are cryptically coloured to avoid detection, the adult is outstandingly marked, so the mother can decoy would-be predators away from her clutch. Loudly calling, she may pretend to have a broken wing to secure the safety of her chicks. Curlews and many other ground-nesting birds share the same tactics.

Insects have a hard external skeleton which does not allow for growth. Immature invertebrates pass through different physical forms before reaching sexual maturity in adulthood. Each phase in the insect's life is fraught with danger from predators. Camouflage is the answer, but it takes on different patterns at every stage in response to the environment. As eggs, the insects must be the right colour and well concealed in a hiding-place that, when the time comes, can also provide food for larvae or caterpillars. Many caterpillars mimic buds or twigs, not only adopting their precise coloration, but also by striking the correct physical attitude on the branch.

When the time comes to pupate, the larvae of the Privet

hawk moth turns brown just before it drops to the earth in order to pass through the stage of metamorphosis in the soil. Insects like the August thorn moth change in colour from brown to green in preparation for pupating among elm leaves. Brazilian butterflies of the Ageronia genus pupate disguised as rolled-up leaves, hanging from the trees in full view of predatory birds and other enemies.

Butterflies have two conflicting needs. The first is to be noticed, so as to attract other butterflies and breed. The second is to avoid being eaten before laying those vital eggs. So butterflies have two coats. With wings outspread, they immediately attract attention, but with wings closed the insect almost disappears. Should a predatory bird such as a kestrel miss its butterfly prey on the first strike, it does not get a second chance because the butterfly flutters to the ground where it resembles just another dried-up leaf.

Some sea-slugs get the pigments they need to blend in with their surroundings from the sponges on which they feed. However, the colours of their relative the sea-hare are determined differently. Starting life in deep water, the sea-hare migrates towards the shore as it gets older, changing colour at every stage, progressing from rose-red to red-brown and ending up a shade of olive-brown. Although the colours match the seaweed on which the sea-hare feeds, the transformation has nothing to do with food, for sea-hares will change colour with age even in the laboratory where the food supply is consistent. Like the colours of juvenile birds, those of the immature sea-hare have been determined over millions of years of evolution and written into its genetic code.

WHITE FOR WINTER

The need to moult their coats gives animals an opportunity to change colours with the season. Many Arctic and sub-arctic species have brown or grey coats in the summer, but adopt white coats in winter. It looks like a straightforward case of camouflage, but all is not as it seems.

Obviously, Arctic and Snowshoe hares, Collared lemmings, Willow grouse and ptarmigan have a natural desire to stay

OPPOSITE PAGE.
Freshly emerged from its pupa case, the Comma butterfly (Polygonia c-album) stretches its wings for the first time. The broken-up shape of the wing edge and the dark coloration of the underside help the butterfly to remain unobserved during its hibernation among old leaves or weathered timbers.

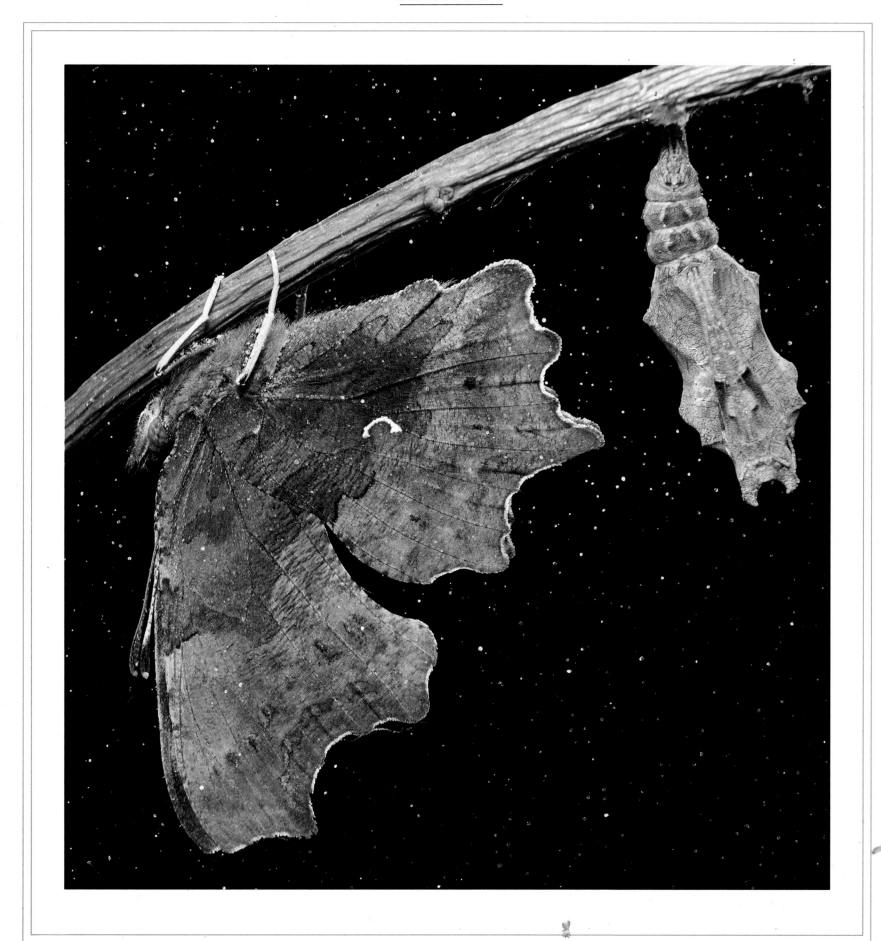

off the menu of their main predators. The trouble is that the Arctic fox, the stoat and the weasel are wearing white coats too. Are both sides in hiding, one to catch and the other to run? The situation is clearly dangerous because nearby the Snowy owl patrols the dark skies on silent wings.

At these latitudes, death comes mainly from the cold. Extra food is required to keep both predator and prey warm during a season when there is little food about, so heat energy must be conserved. Shivering is one way of keeping warm, but a good coat is better. And white coats are the best of all, because whiteness in birds and mammals is really a translucence caused by the absence of melanin. Instead of bulky pigment, numerous air spaces fill the shaft of the hair and the feather barbule. These reflect and scatter light, giving an impression of whiteness. The hollow fibres are immensely light, so the animal can carry a thicker coat with no added weight. But, more important, the hollow white fibres offer better insulation against cold than coloured ones could. Dark birds roost under cover of trees so they can benefit from the back-radiation of their surroundings, but white birds like Snowy owls lose so little heat from their bodies they can afford to roost right out in the open.

One of the things that has puzzled biologists is why the Arctic hares of Ellesmere Island, Baffin Island and Greenland keep their white coats through the summer as well. White reflects all wavelengths of light, so perhaps the colour keeps them cool by day while the hollow fur keeps them warm at night. Whatever the reason, it must be more important than hiding from predators.

Although the use of white as camouflage and insulation is obviously of value, there may be other factors involved. The pigmentation of polar species tends to be reduced; whether predator or prey, they are all lighter in colour than their southern counterparts. Shorter days and colder temperatures induce colour change, but we do not yet know the whole story of why white is right for winter.

CONCEALMENT AND CAMOUFLAGE

There has been extensive research carried out on the optical tricks used for camouflage. Size is no obstacle to camouflage. It is astonishing how inconspicuous elephants can be amongst the sparse and dessicated trees of the African scrub. Whole herds of these large animals can disappear within the space of a minute, their bodies cloaked by the scrappiest of bushes.

The great art of camouflage depends on getting the eye to send messages to the brain in order to build up a meaningless mental image. Camouflage is the product of a struggle between predator and prey. Both sides use it with extraordinary cunning, continually monitoring and responding to the activities of the other. Although it is evolution and not intelligence that is the designer of these colour strategies, it is largely a psychological war.

A frog sees a fly sitting on a wall, but the image is meaningless unless the fly moves. With recognition comes immediate action; within a split second, the frog's sticky tongue has captured the insect. Instinctive behaviour is faster than action stimulated by decision. The payoff is more food. Animals that depend on quick reflexes to catch their prey may not be able to afford the luxury of much intelligence.

Camouflage exploits the errors in identification that animals tend to make if they depend on crude triggers for instinctive recognition. Frogs are not very intelligent, but camouflage fools clever primates like man too. Although we think we see everything around us, our brains are continually making mental short-cuts.

It is important that the coat has the right background colour. In the simplest forms of camouflage, the animal just blends with the overall shades of its environment, so antelopes are basically brown and tree snakes tend to be green. Camouflage may be a better strategy than hiding in holes for animals that are commonly the prey of larger predators. Out in the open, it may at least give them time to run away.

Where evolution has failed to provide a suitable body colour it can be acquired. Certain beetles cover themselves with chalk, sand or mud. The Looper caterpillar is quite naked except for a few hairs which it uses like coathangers for a cryptic wardrobe made out of lichens. This kind of camouflage is called 'adventitious colour resemblance.' The pattern of adornment is usually quite precise. Species of caddis fly larvae can be identified by the style of the protective case they construct and the materials they use to disguise themselves.

Matching their liquid surroundings, some aquatic creatures have become virtually invisible. The Glass catfish, an inhabitant of tropical rivers in Asia, is almost completely transparent. Light passes through the skin and muscles and is reflected off surrounding objects, so the fish is hardly visible. The physiology of this transparency is not understood. When dead, the Glass catfish becomes opaque. There are many jelly-like animals living in mid-ocean. Some, like comb jellies, are trying to avoid being eaten, but the predatory jellyfish use camouflage to go hunting, trying to entrap smaller creatures into their lethal net of almost invisible tentacles.

As well as the overall cryptic colour, the markings or texture of an animal's coat are also crucial to the effectiveness of its camouflage. The stripy orange pelt of the Bengal tiger is surprisingly hard to see in the tropical forests of India where dense shadows contrast with bright shafts of sunlight. Inhabiting open country, its cousin the Siberian tiger wears a plain coat which is equally cryptic. Out on the open savannah, the big cats like the cheetah and leopard have spotted coats which blend softly with their mottled surroundings.

Big cats need camouflage because, although they can move quickly, they cannot run as far or as fast as their fleet-footed prey. Camouflage allows them to creep stealthily up to their victims to make a short dash at top speed for the kill. If a lion does not seize a zebra immediately, the chance is lost and the herd fled. Antelope, wildebeest and zebra are keen to spot predators before they can do any harm. They often ignore lions casually walking or resting nearby because the predator's body language speaks of tranquillity so the prey do not recognize any danger. However, the sight of a lion crouching or sneaking up on the herd will send the potential prey into a stampede. It is the characteristic outline of the hunting lion that triggers the response, not the recognition of the lion as a species.

The position of markings can change the apparent shape of an animal. Distinctive blotches or bands distract the eye from the outline of the animal, while contrasting cryptic shades encourage other parts of the animal's body to blend with the environment. The result is a jumble of optical fragments, the body disintegrated to resemble inanimate objects and mere tricks of the light. Some of the markings may be very prominent, but that does not matter. What is important is that the shape that triggers recognition is changed. The skin of the Gaboon viper is strongly marked and extremely obvious against a plain background, but its colours of black, brown, buff and grey merge exactly with the haphazard shadows and colours of fallen leaves on the forest floor. The triangular black patches divert attention from its head and eyes, so potential prey find it more difficult to recognize the snake and its intentions.

Our eyes are automatically drawn to the eyes of others. That is the effect of concentric circles, and it poses a camouflage problem for animals that would rather not be noticed. Distinctive eyestripes break up the outline of the head and eye to disguise birds such as snipe and woodcock. To hide their dark pupils, some nocturnal snakes, lizards and frogs have changed the shape of the pupil to a thin, horizontal slit. The rest of the eye is cryptically coloured to match the skin. The fish *Petrometopon cruentatus* from Tortugas has developed spots on the skin and the conjunctiva to disguise its round pupil. In most species, eyelids are coloured to match the surrounding body and, when danger threatens, the eye is closed to a slit. The chameleon's eyes, together capable of 360 degree vision, are almost entirely enclosed by skin and only the pupil is ever visible.

The brilliantly coloured Butterfly fish have a special enemy. The Sabre-toothed blennies are carnivorous parasites that feed by biting pieces of skin from larger fish. They are particularly fond of eyes, so the head of the Butterfly fish is boldly marked with a dark stripe to mislead the blenny. Other body markings and a false eye-spot induce the predator to attack the tail instead.

The solid look of an object can be confused by countershading. Normally an object lit from above is paler on top and darker underneath. To counteract this, animals have evolved with darker backs and lighter underbellies. Combined with other forms of camouflage, countershading flattens the image of a three-dimensional object, enabling it to effectively melt into the environment.

Some species of African catfish swim upside-down, so the countershading is reversed and they have dark bellies and lighter backs. The colour-sensitive cuttlefish are able to modify their countershading to fit their orientation in the water. It does not matter which way up the cuttlefish is swimming, the top of its body is always darker. Cuttlefish also use colour for communication and defence. When threatened, they squirt heavily pigmented ink as a protective screen under cover of which they can escape. This ink has a mildly numbing effect which prevents the predator finding its prey by smell.

No matter how exquisitely colour-matched an animal may be to its surroundings, the existence of shadows will prove the camouflage a sham by emphasizing the body shape that millions of years of evolution has sought to hide. Plover chicks cast a shadow that is more noticeable than the softly

Strategically placed on top of the head, the frog's eye gives a wide angle of vision. The iris is cryptically coloured to match the surrounding skin, so the eye is less conspicuous to predators.

speckled nestling itself. So, when their parents sound the alarm, the chicks instinctively crouch low and remain motionless to eliminate their shadows. Plaice alter their body-colour to match their surroundings, but if they did not physically flatten themselves to the seabed, their shadows would give them away. As immature fish, they have a torpedo-shaped body and a symmetrical head like other fish. As they mature and flatten their bodies to live on the seabed, the eyes move round the head to the upper side.

The world's most superbly camouflaged lizard is undoubtedly the Leaf-tailed gecko from Madagascar. A nocturnal hunter, it spends the day pressed head-down against the trunk of a tree in the rainforest. The gecko deals with the problem of shadow by extending a frilly border of skin around the edge of its body and under its head. Drawing its back legs under its tail, it splays its feet against the bark, gripping with rounded, sucker-like toes. Like a chameleon, it can rapidly alter the colour and apparent texture of its skin to blend in with the lichens on the tree trunk. Its large creamy eyes are streaked to match. If it is disturbed, the Leaf-tailed gecko raises its tail like a weapon and opens its large mouth to expose a startlingly bright red tongue.

Inevitably, behaviour patterns have evolved to support all sorts of disguises. When a European bittern is disturbed at the nest, it does not fly away, but lifts its head to align the markings on its neck with the vertical shadows of the surrounding reeds. It will even sway in unison with vegetation that is moving in the wind.

Nightjars hide by keeping perfectly still. Their beautifully subtle flecked plumage ensures that they merge perfectly with the leaf litter as they sleep on the woodland floor during the day. When dusk falls, they are ideally placed to watch out for insects silhouetted against the sky. Keeping still has other advantages. The superbly camouflaged Common poorwill passes the winter in the desert areas of Mexico by going torpid, a state rather like hibernation. This saves a lot of energy, but it is not common behaviour among birds because it leaves them vulnerable to predators.

The pressure behind the evolution of effective camouflage is intense. There is no room for failure. Many creatures are extraordinarily vulnerable and camouflage is their sole defence. The eggs of ground-nesting birds such as lapwings, Ringed plover or Oystercatcher lie on the ground completely exposed, yet they are so well camouflaged that they are indistinguishable from the pebbles. But a Black-backed gull is a very special kind of birdwatcher. Its own survival depends on its vigilance, and it is both opportunistic and aggressive. In the face of such predation, camouflage must be truly excellent if it is to work at all.

If a species is to survive, it is vital that 'failures' should exist. Without the possibility of genetic variation, the species would have no defence against extinction. However, environmental change can throw the best-laid camouflage plans into disarray. In Britain before 1850 the common form of the Peppered moth was a pale insect, nicely camouflaged to blend with the lichens on the bark of its favourite trees. A black, melanistic form was occasionally seen by lepidopterists, but it was rare. The factories that brought wealth during the Industrial Revolution changed the face of the land, as atmospheric pollution coated fields and trees with a fine layer of soot. By 1900, the black form of the Peppered moth accounted for 95 per cent of the population around the city of Manchester. Within the space of fifty years, the white moth had become locally rare.

It was not until the mid-twentieth century that it was proved beyond doubt that bird predation was the cause of this change in population. The correctly camouflaged form survived in large numbers, while the other moths were snapped up by predators. The interaction of predator and prey determined the accuracy of the camouflage, but change was possible because there was genetic variety in the species.

COURTSHIP

Courtship is a highly ritualized procedure for most animals because two things must happen before mating can take place. The female must recognize that the male is her own species and she must become sexually aroused to allow copulation. Because recognition is so crucial, many sexual displays by birds take the form of ritualized preening, which allows the male to show off various distinguishing marks as well as his general vitality. Some male ducks have a distinctive patch of colour on the wing called a speculum. It acts as a visible recognition mark in flight, as well as enhancing sexual display.

Colour signals are an integral part of courtship. There are more than 400 species of vividly coloured cichlid fish in Lake Malawi, many of which look similar to one another. No one has ever seen evolution, but Lake Malawi is a young lake and here you catch its shadow, for scientists are continually discovering new colour morphs and species, especially among the brightly coloured rock-dwelling Mbuna group.

The sheer diversity of similar cichlid life forms makes identifying a suitable mate difficult, so the males display to passing females, exhibiting their colours in a series of movements that is characteristic of the species. Females respond to the ritual and colours of their own species by laying eggs. She does not leave them lying around because other fish might eat them. She picks them up in her mouth. At this point, the male displays his anal fin which is brightly spotted. The colour message is irresistible and the female tries to pick them up as though they were eggs. As she does so, the male releases his milt into her mouth, fertilizing the real eggs. The female carries the brood until they hatch. Some species even brood the baby fish in their mouths.

OPPOSITE PAGE

Until the 1850s, the common form of Peppered moth (Biston betularia) was pale in colour and blended well with lichens on the bark of the trees where the moth rested during the day. The Industrial Revolution in Britain coated the countryside in soot and, fifty years later, the only Peppered moths that could be found near industrial areas were black. Predators had wiped out the white moths before they could breed, changing the dominant colour of the species.

SEXINESS

Colour is exciting and dangerous. Not all males get the chance to mate. In many species, only the strongest individuals pass on their genes. Fighting is one way of determining the fittest, but a breeding strategy that encourages boundless aggression would result in the annihilation of the species, so animals have various ways of avoiding this. Some put all their energies into being sexy. Attracting females by means of an alluring display is safer than fighting over them. It allows young males a chance to compete without the risk of needless injury. Best of all, a successful display can arouse a large number of partners into a sexually receptive condition.

Male birds-of-paradise set up courts in the rain forest where they display their extravagant finery to visiting females, posturing and pirouetting before them in dances of tender avian eroticism. Their feathers are often iridescent and form spectacular capes, pennons, fans and epaulettes. The Emperor bird-of-paradise shows off his cascades by hanging upside-down at the climax of his display. The Magnificent bird-of-paradise carefully prunes the trees to allow a shaft of sunlight into his court to 'spotlight' his strikingly coloured feet, bill and tongue. An iridescent green, the erectile breast shield of the Twelve-wired bird-of-paradise floats above a stunning display of flank-feathers shaped like twisted wires. All this finery is for the delectation of a covey of rather drab females, who do the rounds of several courts in order to choose the most glorious mate.

The birds-of-paradise have few predators, so the males have been free to develop what is undoubtedly the most exotic plumage in the bird kingdom, and they are not afraid to dance in their finery close to the ground. There is plenty of food in New Guinea, so the females have no trouble in rearing their chicks without male assistance. For some species, this leaves the males free to carry on dancing, with the result that they mate with several females, passing on their characteristics to many more clutches. In evolutionary terms, the birds-of-paradise have been most successful in the use of colour to attract and sexually stimulate their females.

In wet areas of northern Europe and Asia, male ruff get together at the beginning of the breeding season to hold their annual lek. The males compete with one another, posturing to display different coloured ruffs of magnificent plumes around the head and neck. Drab females lurk on the edge of the lekking area, coming forward to mate with the males of

their choice. The females then make a nest about three kilometres away, and then rear the young alone.

Role reversal can be found in the animal world. It is the female Red-necked phalarope that sports the bright red feathers and takes the dominant role in courtship. Spinning round and round on the surface of a marshy pool, she attracts a dull-coloured mate for copulation. He attends her while she lays a clutch of four eggs in a mossy nest at the water's edge. Then he takes over, incubating the eggs and rearing the nestlings on his own. As befits the nurturing role, he is cryptically coloured to avoid detection. The female Red-necked phalarope has no need of camouflage. Often as not, she will return to spinning provocatively on her pool in order to attract another mate and lay another clutch of eggs.

Sexual display has its place in monogamous relationships too. Common cranes mate for life, staying together for over thirty years. They certainly do not need display for attraction. Nevertheless their courtship ritual is one of the loveliest dances in the natural world and a necessary prelude to mating. With wings outstretched to display breeding plumage, they prance around each other, throwing their heads back to make magnificent trumpeting calls.

TERRITORY

Colour adds another dimension to the repertoire of behaviour. It can highlight threatening displays to make them more effective. Female chaffinches with breast feathers dyed pink to look like those of the males become dominant over other females. They can even chase males away. A male bird with shabby feathers is more likely to lose control of a prime territory, although it will not prevent him attracting a mate.

The European robin is highly territorial, and will attack any rival that enters its area. The attack is automatic, simply triggered by the sight of red feathers. Experiments have shown that even a stuffed robin will elicit furious song,

OPPOSITE PAGE
Macaws are social birds and their display of vivid colour serves to enhance their solidarity, enabling members of the species to identify each other and avoid interbreeding with other species. A bare patch on the face of the macaw can be flushed pink to indicate arousal or irritation.

aggressive fluffing of breast feathers and eventually enraged pecking by the resident robin. If the dummy robin's feathers are covered with drab paint, the attacks cease, so the colour red *is* the trigger for defensive behaviour. If an invader refuses to flee, the defending robin will actually try to peck him to death. The male robin is not only defending his nest and his mate. The real point of the conflict is to protect the territory so that he and his mate will be able to find enough food to rear a clutch successfully.

The African fish eagle and the American bald eagle both display bright white feathers on the head. The bald eagle, symbol of the United States of America, derives its name from 'balde', the old English world for white. The head of this bird is so distinctive that an incubating bird sitting on a nest can be seen from afar. It is as though the white head acts like a flag, marking the exact site of a nest so the other fish eagles can avoid the nesting territory. Both bald eagles and their close relatives the African fish eagles, will drive away intruders who ignore the message.

JUVENILE DISPLAY

Hungry nestlings wave brightly coloured gapes at their parents, all the time shrilly piping as they compete with each other for a share of the food. The intense colour of the throat lining acts as a signal to the parents. Birds that nest in burrows have particularly bright throats that display shades of orange, yellow or white as guides for the parents. The throat of the Gouldian finch is even decorated with glistening 'beads' which glow in the dark.

The Eurasian cuckoo is usually much bigger than the species it parasitizes. There is no competition with the legitimate clutch, because the baby cuckoo ejects rival hatchlings from the nest straight away. However, to ensure a sufficient supply of food, the cuckoo has a particularly bright red gape which stimulates its foster-parents into bringing more and more food until they are almost dropping from exhaustion.

Colour plays an important role in the relationship between adult and juvenile gulls. The adults have a bright orange spot on their bills. After the eggs have hatched, the parent birds bring food to the chicks, carried in the throat, and wait until the nestlings peck at the orange spot on their bill. This action stimulates the parent bird into regurgitating the food for the chicks to eat.

MIMICRY

A large number of animals mimic inanimate objects like leaves and twigs for defence. Silk moth caterpillars are extraordinarily adept at disguising themselves, their bodies following the leaf structure of their favourite foodplants. The South American Leaf fish floats, apparently no more than a scrap of waterlogged vegetation, in the vegetation, in the forest streams of the River Amazon. Its body is leaf-shaped – and it even has a stalk! The Leaf fish is a voracious predator, not hiding but hunting. It is able to swallow large prey up to half the size of its own body, and it can adjust its colour and markings to match the changing colours of the real leaves that float all around.

The skin of a crocodile is deeply fissured to resemble a log. It is so natural for dead wood to be floating at the edge of a river that animals take no notice as they come to drink. This makes it simple for the crocodile to seize quite large prey, dragging it underwater to drown. The strategy of mimicry has defined and limited the crocodile's hunting technique and it has the equipment to do nothing else, but as long as its prey need to drink, the crocodile will not go hungry.

Although the Eurasian cuckoo parasitizes over 100 species of birds, its eggs are closely marked to resemble those of the chosen host. Individual cuckoos seem to specialize – or adopt – particular species, but are prepared to branch out and lay eggs in other nests if the opportunity presents itself.

Laying fifteen eggs or more each season, each in a different nest, 138 species of cuckoo all around the world have discovered that they can produce far more young using mimicry than they could possibly rear unaided. In an effort to distinguish the nestlings, the gapes of young Bearded tits or reedling have evolved an eye-catching pattern of white fleshy projections on a black and red background. Cuckoos are already developing similar gape markings of their own, but the reedling have succeeded, for a while, in reducing the success of their old enemy.

OPPOSITE PAGE
Not just cryptically coloured, but shaped to be almost indistinguishable from the environment, the stick insect's body mimics the dry grass stems in which it feeds.

Mimicry can be used by the victim too. The Californian blue-tailed skink has developed an eye-catching tail. Like that of many other diurnal lizards, it breaks off and wriggles vigorously for a while if it is seized by a predator, giving the skink time to escape. The tail regenerates quickly, and surveys show large numbers of lizards regrowing their tails, so it seems the strategy is effective.

The Common potoo hunts by night along the woodland streams of the West Indies and north eastern South America, scooping up insects on the wing. By day, this unusual bird roosts in a tree, where it sits perfectly camouflaged against the bark. If it is disturbed, the potoo stiffens, raising its head so that its body shape and plumage markings resemble a broken branch. The Tawny frogmouth in Australia has adopted a similar strategy. This master of disguise roosts by day, resting on the branch of a tree where its mottled grey plumage is indistinguishable from the bark.

MIMICRY AND COMMUNICATION

The language of colour is extremely powerful and impossible to ignore. As a result, many animals have developed strategies for communication that involve mimicry. Several species of monkeys have a red penis and a bright blue scrotum which they exhibit conspicuously to drive away rival males from other groups. This potent message is reproduced in an identical colour pattern on the face of the mandrill, where it acts as a threat signal in a similar way. Low-ranking male Hamadryas baboons have genitals that are colour-marked to mimic those of the females. To appease the aggressive alpha male, they present them in a pseudo-sexual display to indicate subservience. Colour is important to these primates. Female baboons display large perineal swellings to let males know when they are in oestrus, and pregnancy in baboons is signalled by a reddening of the rump.

TRAPS

Cryptic camouflage and mimicry may combine to create energy-saving hunting techniques. Predators that lie in wait for their victims often imitate objects that are attractive to their prey. The Malaysian Flower-mantis is shaped and tinted to resemble the flowers on which its insect prey feeds. As a flower-mimic, the mantis runs less risk of being eaten itself by insectivorous birds than it would if it rested on a leaf.

Crab spiders are an inventive family. Imitating a bird dropping, the Malaysian crab spider preys on butterflies and other insects that like to feed on the salts found in bird excrement. The crab spider's imitation is hard to distinguish from the real thing. It even spins a thin film of web around itself to imitate the white, liquid part of the dropping.

Perhaps the most macabre mimic of all is the cichlid fish *Haplochromis livingstoni* which lives in Lake Malawi. Feigning death, it floats slightly sideways near the bottom, taking on the greenish mottle hues of decomposition. There are many small carnivorous fish among the rock-dwelling Mbuna of Lake Malawi, and they are easily lured to investigate, then caught and eaten.

Carnivores generally feed on animals smaller than themselves, but in the sea there are many fish living in close or symbiotic relationship with larger fish. One of the most interesting is the Cleaner-wrasse, which has formed a mutually beneficial arrangement with large fish that need to rid themselves of ectoparasites. Wearing distinctive colours to identify themselves, the Cleaner-wrasse work in pairs, allowing client-fish to visit their territory for an intimate service which may include dental care. Queues sometimes form around the edge of the territory and this has given the Sabre-toothed blenny its chance. Even the most aggressive large fish relax while they are being cleaned. The blenny imitates the 'uniform' of the Sea swallow or Blue streak blenny to approach its victim, taking a painful bite before making good its escape.

The angler fish have a particularly crafty way of saving energy and catching food at the same time. Bottom-dwelling species flatten and camouflage themselves to merge with the seabed. A frill of scales breaks up their outlines, which are marked in cryptic colours. The only visible parts are the eyes strategically placed on top of the head. A fleshy lure held on the end of a filament, rather like a small fishing-rod, projects from the head. In dark, deep water the lure is luminescent, and fascinated prey are drawn to it, dangling just above the angler fish's cavernous mouth.

Any device which deflects attack – even if only occasionally – becomes enshrined in the genetic code if the animal manages to breed before succumbing to predation. Many insects have discovered that they can 'shock' a predator into leaving them alone by suddenly displaying bright colours or a false eye. Geckos open their mouths suddenly to threaten with a bright red gape, while the Australian frilled lizard suddenly increases its apparent size in response to threat by erecting an enormous ruff as it opens its mouth. Tropical frogs and toads have even developed brightly coloured false eyes on their thighs which imply the presence of a much larger animal to frighten away predators.

WARNING COLORATION

Butterflies seem so vulnerable. Their bright, attractive colours are deliberately conspicuous so they must employ other strategies to survive. Those that advertise themselves in shades of bright red, orange, white and black are often unpleasant-tasting, their bodies loaded with toxic chemicals. Insectivorous birds, mammals and reptiles soon learn that certain distinctive patterns or colour combinations are to be avoided. Butterflies are able to rely on the learned behaviour of predators for their survival.

Today, there are many butterflies and countless moths armed with a sophisticated range of chemical weapons. White butterflies taste unpleasant because the white coloration is made from a waste product of metabolism called pterin. Closely related to uric acid, pterins are similar to the substance that makes bird droppings white. To make their wings taste even nastier, white butterflies also absorb mustard oil glycosides from cabbage leaves. The American Monarch butterfly stores cardiac glycosides in its body. These are heart poisons similar to digitalis, which are obtained by the caterpillars from the milkweed plant.

Poison can be delivered in a number of ways. Wasps and bees are armed with stings which are really modified ovipositors or egg ducts. A number of caterpillars are very hairy, and on insects like the Flannel-moth caterpillar from

Central America, the hairs connect with a poison gland at their base. In Brazil, the Flannel-moth caterpillars are known as *bizos de fuero* ('fire beasts') because the extremely irritant poison can cause pain and paralysis in sensitive people which can last for weeks. The vividly marked black and yellow Arrow poison frog secretes poisonous chemicals through its skin to deter predators. South American Indians collect the substance and make a concentrate in which they dip the tips of their arrows. In this form, the substance is one of the most deadly of venoms.

Poisons are an integral part of the defence systems of countless animals, from scorpions to sea-slugs. It is not surprising therefore, to find that many harmless animals, who are unable to tolerate the poisons themselves, find it advantageous to look as if they are dangerous or unpleasant-tasting. For example, the deadly Brazilian Coral snake has an almost identical mimic, a non-poisonous member of the *Colubridae* family.

The strong colour combination of yellow and black is the stamp of identity that sets apart the hornets, wasps and bees. These straightforward warning colours are seldom ignored twice. For this reason, it makes excellent cover for many species of non-stinging insects that wish to be left alone by birds. The mimicry is often very precise because birds have excellent eyesight and are quick to weed out the obvious fakes from the insect population.

THE PSYCHOLOGY OF COLOUR

Our perception of the way in which colour works in the natural world is conditioned by our human experiences and emotions. Colour cannot be properly described in words, although we share the perception with every other human being. The feelings that are associated with colour are universal to human beings, but much of it is subliminal. We are not consciously aware of being manipulated by crimson lips; we are out of conscious touch with the part of the brain that handles these perceptions. Because we have constructed an artificial environment that protects us from the life and death struggles of the natural world, we no longer use the language of colour as a survival technique.

In studying animals we have to look at life from their point of view. While we might associate the colour orange with the cosy warmth of a fireside other creatures may put a different interpretation on it, such as 'sex' or 'bushfire'. Unusual colours or patterns may carry psychological messages of life-or-death importance.

The stripes on the coat of a zebra make it one of the most eye-catching animals in the natural world. In the past, biologists have tried to explain it away by pointing out that the stripes break up the outline of the zebra at a distance. If it is true that the stripes are cryptic camouflage, then it is one of the worst attempts at hiding in the animal kingdom.

Alternative theories suggest that the stripes are useful in deterring insects from biting, and that a vividly stripy animal is harder to catch because it deceives the eye of the predator. Nothing has been proved.

However, it is known that several types of primary nerve cells in the visual system are excited by crisp black and white images. Living in a herd, zebra are continually experiencing this visual stimulation and they seem to like it. If a captive zebra is presented with a board painted black and white, it will sidle up to it in a friendly way. It knows the board is a board, but it may be that stripes produce some chemical in the brain that makes the zebra feel relaxed and comfortable.

Zebra are the main prey of lions and will scatter in all directions when chased, not stopping until they are sure they are safe. It often takes days for the herd to regroup and this may be too long for mothers in search of their foals. A stripy beacon, one that can be seen over a long distance, may help the herd to gather together again and encourage frightened youngsters to seek out their mothers.

BRAIN AND INTERPRETATION

Colour, it seems, affects animals directly, by-passing intellectual thought-processes to instigate action as a reflex. It does this by acting on the emotions of fear and attraction, playing on feelings of aggression and security.

Even jellyfish are sensitive to light, and both birds and insects have better colour vision than human beings, but their response to this information is strictly limited by the use their brains can make of the information. Higher animals with more complex and integrated neural equipment are not only aware of changes in their surroundings but are equipped to make decisions based on this information.

However, the repertoire of instinctive responses which served these creatures so well at earlier stages in their evolution is not lost. Instinctive responses are faster than considered ones. A fox does not think twice before responding to a rustle in the grass with a pounce. In fact, it does not think at all. Conscious thinking is a time-wasting and energy-draining activity. Even the human brain is programmed to avoid doing it, for it sets up suitable automatic responses to replace decision-making whenever possible. If it did not, we should be unable to learn complex skills such as driving a car. In humans, two types of brain activity handle colour, one instinctive and the other intellectual. We are aware of the intellectual apparatus, but less conscious of the instinctive interpretations which are characteristic of the animal world.

Animal responses to colour are neat short-circuiting devices to trigger specific behaviour. It is 'mindless', but millions of years of evolution ensure that it works. Colour strategy is a basic response to environment. Refined by thousands, maybe millions of generations, colour signals have proved a reliable aid to defence and hunting, a powerful way of establishing territory, a delightful form of courtship and an excellent alternative to male violence.

Humans also use colour strategy to serve a variety of purposes. We use warning coloration to direct traffic, we apply sexual colours in the form of make-up and we construct attractive images to sell goods and services. It may be that the appreciation of art in a gallery or museum is a way of bringing certain subliminal activities of the brain, like colour perception, into the area of conscious thought. Colour speaks directly to the spirit in a secret language of which the human mind is only distantly aware.

OPPOSITE PAGE
*One of the largest of all moths, the wingspan of the female
Atlas moth* (Attacus atlas) *may span 25.4 cm (10 in). At rest,
the tawny markings hide the insect from predatory birds.
However, should a bird show unwanted interest, the Atlas
moth can open its wings suddenly to expose distinctive
triangular markings that may surprise the bird into flight.*

THE CAUSE OF COLOUR

White light is composed of all the colours of the rainbow. When it falls on a coloured object containing pigment, some wavelengths are absorbed and others reflected. The colour that we see as a result represents the sum total of the reflected wavelengths. White and blue are not caused by pigments but created by the scattering of light by tiny particles. Called 'Tyndall scattering', it sometimes occurs in conjunction with pigmentary colours to create the brightest shades of green in the animal kingdom.

Iridescence is a form of colour trickery. The colours shimmering on the back of a crow's wing are not really there at all. They are caused by a conflict between wavelengths reflected back from the glossy surface of the feather and those reflected from the pigment layer beneath. Overlapping, the two wavelengths 'fight', partially cancelling each other out.

A large number of animals have evolved the ability to change colour to match their surroundings. Rapid colour changes like those of the chameleon or the octopus imply an acute sensitivity to the colours of the environment. Curiously, the octopus does not see colour with its eyes, but senses it through special pores in the skin.

OPPOSITE PAGE *Refracted by raindrops, white light is split into the colours of the visible light spectrum to create the rainbow. Each colour represents a different vibration, ranging from the warm, long wavelengths of red and orange, through yellow and green, to the cold, short wavelengths of blue, indigo and purple.*

Plants that have evolved to use birds to spread their pollen generally produce red flowers to attract the birds. The eyesight of birds such as this Broad-billed hummingbird (Cyanthus latirostris) is extremely sensitive to red wavelengths.

LEFT ABOVE AND BELOW *Male birds-of-paradise set up individual 'courts' in the forest during the breeding season. Plain brown females visit several courts to watch a flamboyant display designed to show off the male's fine feathers. The metallic hues of the breast feathers of the male Blue bird-of-paradise (Philodris magnifica) are caused by the interference colours of iridescence.*

Bioluminescence is rare on land. These rainforest fungi may be glowing to attract insects to spread its spores. Bioluminscence is the result of the chemical reaction of a substance – generally luciferin – with an enzyme called a luciferase.

LEFT *As juveniles, plaice* (Pleuronectes platessa) *are midwater swimming fish with eyes placed normally on either side of the head. As they mature, they change both colour and shape as they flatten themselves laterally to take up residence on the seabed. Half-buried in sand, mud or gravel, they adopt the colour and texture of the environment. The lower eye migrates around the top of the head to establish itself next to the other in a more useful position.*

Cave glowworms (Arachnocanda luminosa) *stream out of their roost into the night. Bioluminescence enables glowworms to find each other and may have other social functions in this species.*

RIGHT *A female glowworm* (Lampyris noctiluca) *swings her body to and fro to create a strobe effect with her bioluminescent tail. Although the speck of light is tiny, the eyesight of male glowworms is sensitive. The pulse of the female's bioluminescence is irresistible and males will be drawn from a wide area.*

Cocking its head to get a good look, the Cassowary (Casuarius unappendiculatus) is angling its eye to direct light on to a specially sensitive area on the retina. Called the fovea, this part of the retina is rich in cones, giving the bird telescopic or close-up vision which helps it to locate insects and small vertebrates on the forest floor.

The compound eye of insects like the housefly gives extremely good definition as well as a large angle of vision. Most insects have more sophisticated eyesight than humans, for they are sensitive to short wavelengths and can see the ultra-violet colours of plants which are invisible to us.

Famous for changing colour quickly, chameleons are also adept at
using subtle colours to imitate the texture of their surroundings.
The bulbous head of this High-casqued chameleon combined with
the frill under the chin alter the outline of the animal making it
hard to distinguish amongst foliage.

RIGHT *The Cape dwarf chameleon is showing skin containing a
Tyndall blue scattering layer alongside orange melanin pigment
held in chromatophore cells. The green is created by an oily yellow
layer of skin lying over the blue.*

The largest of the parrots, the Hyacinth macaw (Anodorrhynchus hyacinthinus) *from South America can grow to a height of 100 cm (39 in). Its cobalt-blue coloration is the result of a Tyndall blue scattering layer over a dark melanin pigment deep in the feather. Sadly, its vivid colour has proved its downfall, for the Hyacinth macaw has been endangered by the international pet-trade. It is thought only 2,000 birds survive in Brazil.*

The *Sulphur-breasted toucan* (Ramphastos sulfuratus) *combines yellow pigment layers in the skin and the horn of the beak with an underlying Tyndall blue scattering layer to create creamy-green and blue hues. The tip of the bill is coloured by a red pigment.*

Pigments in the feather give the Himalayan monal pheasant (Lophophorus impejanis) its red, brown and yellow hues. Blue is created by the reflection of light from a scattering layer of particles. Where these combine with pigment layers in the feather, hues of purple, turquoise and green are created. The feathers are glossy; in strong sunlight, this produces an iridescent shimmer.

LEFT Females can be hard to spot, but the feathers of male pheasants make them conspicuous. These are the breast feathers of the Common pheasant (Phasianus colchicus). There is a variety of differently coloured races and colour forms.

CAMOUFLAGE

Camouflage is useful to hunter and prey alike. It is a better strategy for life than hiding in holes because it gives every victim a chance of last-minute escape. Prey animals cannot afford to spend too much time hiding because they must eat; camouflage enables them to combine the two activities. Predators such as lion and cheetah depend on camouflage for hunting. The only way to catch antelope or zebra is to stalk the herd as the prey are always alert to danger. In the natural world, camouflage is used by both sides, a war of clever shading and subtle coloration in the daily battle for survival. The outline of an animal gives its presence away, so many creatures have evolved strong patterns to confuse the predator by misleading the eye. Combined with cryptic colours on other parts of the body, these strong patterns change the apparent outline of the animal. The image becomes meaningless, so the predator ignores it.

The environment and death are the great driving forces behind evolution. Where camouflage has become important to the survival of a species, only individuals with the most accurate disguise will live to breed. As poor specimens are weeded out, the camouflage improves with the generations. The distribution of dark Peppered moths in industrial areas shows that a wide variety of colour forms may arise continually, but that pressure from predators ensures that only the effectively camouflaged form survives. It is important that 'wrong' colours occur randomly, for this protects the species against extinction should the environment change.

OPPOSITE PAGE *Pronounced brows over the eyes hide the pupils of the Horned frog* (Megophrys nasuta) *and flatten the head so the body resembles a fallen leaf. Defensive camouflage works by confusing the observer, often tricking it into ignoring its prey.*

Butterflies carry both cryptic and flamboyant colours. With wings outstretched, the brilliant social signals of the Large tortoiseshell (Nymphalis polychloros) *are revealed.*

*The wings of the Large tortoiseshell can be shut away in an instant
when danger threatens. With closed wings, the butterfly looks just
like a withered leaf.*

The Snowshoe or Varying hare (Lepus americanus) *is an animal of the sub-arctic forests of North America. Normally brown, it turns white in winter, gaining extra warmth as well as camouflage from its lighter coat.*

RIGHT *White all the year round, polar bears* (Thalarctos maritimus) *spend their winters hibernating in icy caves. They have no need to fear other predators but their cryptic camouflage is useful when hunting for seals on the snowfields or pack ice.*

The Double-crested basilisk (Brasilisans plumifrons) *is an iguana from South America. Likely targets for hungry birds, their banded tails may help them escape capture by distracting the predator's attention away from their heads.*

*A master of camouflage, the Leaf-tailed gecko (Uroplates
fimbriatus) from the rainforests of Madagascar adopts the texture
as well as the colour of the tree trunks. Shadows cast by the
tropical sun are hidden by an irregular frill of skin around the body.*

Thick white fur protects the Arctic fox (Atopex lagopus) from the cold as well as offering cryptic camouflage against the deep snow. The hair shafts of white fur contain hollow pockets where melanin pigment would normally lie. This makes the coat intrinsically warmer. As it is also lighter, the Arctic fox can carry a thicker coat for the same weight.

LEFT *Arctic foxes on Greenland, Ellesmere Island and Baffin Island stay white all year round. In summer they are extremely conspicuous. White reflects all wavelengths of light so the colour white keeps the fox cool during the arctic summer day, and the super-insulation of the fur keeps it warm at night.*

Fallen leaves are the perfect disguise for small animals. Hiding out
in the open rather than in a predictable hole, a moth imitates a leaf
to rest undisturbed through the daylight hours.

RIGHT *Feeding among hazel leaves, the camouflage of a
Brimstone butterfly* (Gonepteryx rhamni) *makes it virtually
invisible. Like the petals of the flowers they visit, the wings of male
and female butterflies are distinguished by ultra-violet markings
– colours beyond the sensitivity of the human eye.*

Stripes are clearly important to zebras. It has been suggested that the bold stripes may break up their outline at a distance, acting as a form of camouflage; but it is also likely that the stripes have a social purpose, helping to keep the herd together.

LEFT *Boldly marked and yet perfectly camouflaged, the tiger's skin is hard to distinguish amongst the light and shadow of tall grasses. In the forest, the stripes combine with the tiger's lean form to make it almost invisible in the tangle of undergrowth.*

Ptarmigan (Lagopus leucurus) *grow white feathers as camouflage through the winter. When spring comes, the females moult back into brown plumage so as to be inconspicuous while sitting on eggs. Males retain their white feathers for a few weeks longer, possibly so that they may decoy predators away from the nest.*

Nightjars (Caprimulgus europaeus) *sit so tight on their nests that
intruders must almost step on them before they will fly away.
Camouflaged to imitate dry leaf-litter, their dark markings
simulate the shadows of the forest floor.*

Flatfish (Bothus podus) *change colour slowly, but they have*
evolved to imitate not only the colour, but also the texture
of the sea floor.

LEFT *As it matures, the Sea-hare* (Aplysia punctatus) *swims*
inshore, gradually changing colour from red to olive-brown.
Although it matches the seaweed on which it feeds, the
transformation has nothing to do with food, for Sea-hares will
change colour with age even in an aquarium.

Yellow spots on a bright green background hardly seems like ideal camouflage colours, but this Graceful chameleon (Chamaeleo gracilis) is perfectly hidden in the dappled sunlight of a leafy bush. Colour change is not only geared to the environment but to the chameleon's emotional state. Female chameleons frequently take on bright colours when they are about to lay eggs.

RIGHT *Warming up, this Three-horned chameleon (Chamaeleo jacksoni) adopts a dark body colour which absorbs the warm wavelength of sunlight more efficiently than a pale colour could.*

One of the most dangerous of fish on a tropical reef, the Stonefish
(Synanceja) lurks in shallow water where its rough and warty skin
resembles the algal growths covering the coral nearby. A sharp
spine armed with toxic venom is hidden in the dorsal fin.

*Cuttlefish can change colour to suit the environment more rapidly
than any other animal. The Giant cuttlefish from Western
Australia grows up to 8 m (26 ft) long and has ten arms.
It senses the colour of its surroundings through its skin.*

Posture as well as colour can be used for disguise. This treesnake has the fresh colours of a newly sprouted shoot. Its pointed head, held at an angle, looks like a bud or leaf.

LEFT *Climbing among the twigs of a withered shrub, the stick insect* (Extatosoma tiaratum) *imitates the dessicated leaves with the irregular appendages on its legs and body.*

FLAMBOYANT DISPLAY

The mating season is a time when animals display their finest feathers, their glossiest fur. Some adopt breeding colours or costume. Special colours to indicate maturity and sexual prowess are helpful to females looking for a mate; they will not waste time with immature males. Markings may serve to cement the pair bond and many animals mate for life, staying with the same partner and ignoring all others.

Mating is often preceded by some kind of courtship dance or ritual. This is an opportunity for males to display certain distinguishing marks to the female who needs reassurance that she is dallying with the right species. Recognition may also be triggered by song or certain characteristic movements, but colour remains the most important stimulus. Although bright colours make them conspicuous and therefore vulnerable to predators, males must take this risk if they are to breed.

The bright colours of breeding plumage may have evolved originally as a form of male communication. Males usually compete with each other for females. To avoid fighting and the attendant risks of injury, males learned to 'read' each other's body language and, by observing plumage and posture, to assess the relative strength of their opponent. Where competition is most fierce, the flamboyant display of males often dominates courtship behaviour.

OPPOSITE PAGE *Iridescent colours enhance the extraordinary display of the male peacock* (Pavo crosatus). *Competition to mate has resulted in extremely long feathers which are folded neatly back when not required.*

Highly aggressive, the Robin (Erithacus rubecula) is enraged by the colour red. During the breeding season he protects his territory fiercely, driving off any other males who challenge him. The red breast is a powerful trigger for Robins to fight. Males with dull feathers are left alone.

The enormously enlarged red pincers of the Fiddler crab are as much a flag as a weapon, marking the immediate territory around the crab's hole. Combat is usually a ritual of claw-waving rather than a real battle. The size of the red claw is also important in attracting a mate.

Like most primates, male vervet monkeys (Cercopithecus aethiops) are aggressive, although genuine fights are usually avoided. They threaten males from rival groups by displaying enlarged and brightly coloured genitals at them. The eye-catching red penis and perineum are set off against an electric blue scrotum.

LEFT Several species of monkeys expose brightly coloured genitals when threatening members of rival groups. Mandrills (Mandrillis sphynx) have adopted the same colour pattern on their faces, adding extra aggression to eye contact.

Male birds-of-paradise compete fiercely with each other for females, setting up individual 'courts' where they perform a combination of dance and acrobatics designed to show off their magnificent plumes to best advantage. The dance of the Emperor bird-of-paradise (Paradisaea guilielmi) *is complicated: he twists, rustles and pirouettes, finally turning upside down to display stunning tail feathers.*

The red gular pouch of the male Frigate bird acts to attract females as well as signalling a threat to other males. Frigate birds nest communally, and the male advertizes his possession of a nest by inflating his throat pouch to enormous dimensions.

RIGHT ABOVE *A male Capercaillie* (Tetrao urogallus) *displays its breeding feathers on the traditional lekking ground by fanning its tail, stamping its feet and emitting a loud booming call.*

RIGHT BELOW *The drab peahen seems mesmerized by the overpowering tail feathers of the peacock. The feathers also act as a screen, diverting her attention from rival males who may be displaying nearby.*

Male birds find it easier to identify a mate than female birds because the former generally imprint on their mothers immediately after hatching. Females depend far more on distinctive markings as sexual signals. The brilliant blue feet of the Blue-footed booby (Sule nebouxii) clearly identifies the species.

RIGHT Female hamadrayas baboons (Papio hamadryas) live in harems closely guarded by a dominant male with whom they may have a relationship that lasts for years. When she comes into oestrus, the perineum of the female swells and turns bright red.

The male ruffs (Philomachus pugnax) *displaying near the centre of the courtship arena are the most attractive to females visiting the lek. In an attempt to hold this key position, the males raise their neck feathers and dance until exhausted.*

LEFT *Although secretive forest birds, male Golden pheasants* (Chrysolophus pictus) *by nature display gaudy feathers and a long tail to attract females. Their plumage is so elaborate, with display structures and spurs, that it may compromise their safety. However, dull-coloured birds are unattractive to females and seldom get the chance to mate and pass on their genes.*

It is the Red-necked phalerope female (Phalaropus lobatus) *that sports the colourful feathers during courtship. Spinning round and round on the water, she entices the male to mate. Then she leaves him to incubate the eggs and raise the young while she courts another male.*

LEFT *The male Three-spined stickleback* (Gasterosteus aculeatus) *adopts a red belly and blue body to advertize his nest to passing females. He may induce several of these females to lay their eggs in the nest; thereafter his bright colours serve to warn other males to keep away.*

BABY COLOURS

Newborn animals need to stimulate their parents to provide protection and
food. Many factors are involved. Scent is important, but colour too plays
a part. Nestlings open their beaks as wide as possible as they beg
for food, exposing a bright red gape which is an irresistible signal
to the adult to feed them.
Camouflage coloration is often vital to the survival of young animals. In the
first few days of life, helpless youngsters such as fawns are often left hidden
while the parent feeds, their spotted coats disguising their presence in
the dappled undergrowth. Insects pass through several growth stages
on the path to maturity. As they form the mainstay of the diet of
many animals, camouflage is vital for eggs as well as larvae and pupae.
The only exceptions are those insects which wear bright colours to
advertize themselves as bad-tasting.

OPPOSITE PAGE *The gapes of nestlings are generally bright red to
stimulate the parent to bring food. Evolution has endowed the
Bearded tit nestlings* (Panurus biarmicus) *with distinctive throat
markings which have developed as a defence against cuckoos. The
parent birds will only feed youngsters with precisely the right
patterns. However, as the only cuckoos to successfully parasitize
the tits must have patterned throats, evolution is even-handedly
ensuring that the cuckoo population develops identical marking.*

Young Lesser black-backed gulls (Larus luseus) *peck at the bright orange spot on the bill to stimulate their parent to regurgitate food. Both male and female bring food to the youngsters and this behaviour ensures that they usually feed only their own offspring.*

*Hatching soon after the snow melts, the extraordinary fluffy
feathers of the Snowy owl (Nyctea scandiaca) chicks are excellent
insulation as well as cryptic camouflage.*

Although the red throat and belly of the male Three-spined
stickleback (Gasterosteus aculeatus) is a breeding display, it is
useful later when the male is guarding the nest and hatchlings. The
young sticklebacks are virtually colourless to evade detection,
while the bright colours of the parent warn other fish away.

LEFT The legitimate young of the Reed warbler have been
supplanted by a cuckoo (Cuculus canorus) chick. Much larger in
size, its appetite is voracious. The immature cries and open gape
are strong signals which the adult Reed warblers cannot ignore, so
they continue to feed the usurper although they know there is
something amiss.

Laid directly on the ground, the eggs of the Killdeer (Charadrius vocifer) are almost impossible to spot among the stones. A nest is not required for shelter and would just attract unwanted attention.

RIGHT *While Killdeer eggs and chicks lie nearby, cryptically camouflaged to evade detection, the parent bird lures predators away from her family with an insistent 'broken wing' display. Fluttering apparently helplessly, she dips and turns, staying just out of reach until the interloper has been lured well away from the breeding area.*

For the first few days after birth the Roe deer fawn is left lying in the undergrowth while the mother feeds nearby. If danger threatens, the fawn freezes, relying on its speckled camouflage for protection while the adults run away, acting as a decoy.

LEFT *The white rump of the Roe deer* (Capreolus capreolus) *is used as a warning signal to other members of the herd. When one member of the herd is alarmed it tells the others by lifting its tail and expanding its white rump as it flees. The signal is irresistible and the whole group instinctively follows.*

Wild boar (Sus scrofa) *seldom leave their offspring undefended for a moment for the succulent piglets would quickly be the target of predators such as wolves. The stripy coats of the babies may be a form of camouflage, as they blend with the dappled lightings of the woodland glades where wild boar generally forage.*

RIGHT *The soft fur of babyhood is often a different colour from the pelt of the adult. Young Red fox* (Vulpes vulpes) *cubs are born with dark brown fur. As the cubs mature, the colour lightens to bright rufous red. As the Red fox is largely nocturnal, the conspicuous colour does not seem to be deterimental to survival.*

TRICKS AND TRAPS

It is an exhausting business chasing prey! The energy expended by the predator during the chase may not equal the calorific content of the kill. How much better it would be if the prey – like the silly goose in the folk story – came to dinner willingly.

It is a short step from camouflage to cunning trickery. Imitating a bird dropping, a Crab spider uses its own body as bait for insects that like to feed on the salts in bird excrement. Flower mantis take the form of the flowers of the plant on which they lurk, and unsuspecting insects land on the mantis as readily as the real blossom.

To deter predators, many insects carry poisons in their bodies to make them distasteful. Warning colours make these insects conspicuous as evolution has worked out a cunning plan that shelters a large number of unpleasant as well as innocuous insects from attack. Predators are not born with an inbuilt knowledge of which animals taste nasty – they have to find out by trial and error. So, to educate them, a small number of brightly coloured insects die. The digestive experience is usually enough to establish a connection between the warning coloration and personal distress that lasts a lifetime. Under the umbrella of this strategy, some species of non-toxic insects have developed similar warning coloration so that they may benefit from the aversion of 'educated' predators.

OPPOSITE PAGE *Caterpillars of the cinnebar moth* (Callimorpha jacobaeae) *carry poisons which they obtain from their food plants. Like most poisonous insects, they are strikingly marked as a last-minute warning to birds. Here the cinnebar moth caterpillars are feeding on ragwort, a plant that is highly poisonous to cattle and horses.*

The trees of the rain forest drip with lichen, and it is an effective shelter for vast numbers of insects. This moth from Costa Rica has adopted the subtle colours and ragged form of the lichen in perfect mimicry.

Seeking to shock its predator into flight, the Owl butterfly (Caligo memnon) has developed large spots on its wings that resemble eyes. When exposed suddenly, the 'eyes' give the impression of a large and possibly dangerous animal that has been disturbed.

Adopting the colour of the flower in which it lurks, a Crab spider (Misumena vatia) *waits to ambush butterflies and other insects that come to feed on the nectar. The flowering season of most plants is short, so Crab spiders must change colour when they move to another plant species.*

RIGHT *The body of the Flower-mantis* (Pseudocreobotra wahlbergi) *so closely resembles the form and colour of a flower that insects are enticed to settle on it – with fatal results!*

This species of Assassin bug has changed its body shape to imitate the narrow waist and swollen abdomen of an ant. It is advantageous for unpleasant-tasting species to mimic each other as it leads to the rapid education of their mutual enemies who – after one nasty experience – tend to leave them all alone.

LEFT *As they fly about, displaying the attractive sexual colours on their wings, butterflies are under constant threat from birds. It is a risk they must run if they are to breed. The Hairstreak butterfly of the Thecla species reduces the death-rate by the use of a false head on the edge of the wing. Attackers may seize the wing instead of the body of the butterfly.*

Mangrove forests are a rich feeding-ground for fish and this
batfish (Platax vespertilio) has evolved among the mangrove roots
disguised as a leaf for protection against predators.

RIGHT The Cleaner wrasse (Labroides dimidiatus) feeds on
parasites and dead skin which it cleans off larger fish like this
Flame dwarf angelfish. The symbiotic relationship is exploited by
a predator called the Sabre-toothed blenny which takes advantage
of its close resemblance to the wrasse to bite chunks out of
unsuspecting 'clients'.

Hairy caterpillars (Dasychira pudibunda) *frequently carry highly irritant poisons, some of which can cause excruciating pain or even temporary paralysis in humans. When thousands of caterpillars display together, fragments of their tiny hairs are carried on the wind and can cause breathing difficulties.*

LEFT *Many caterpillars are camouflaged to resemble the plants on which they feed. This geometrid moth goes even further, assuming a rigid posture against the stem of the plant in order to mimic a twig.*

*The dot on the tail of this Blue-blotched butterflyfish
(Tetrachaetodon plebius) resembles an eye, and it distracts the
predator from the fish's head. A fraction of a second of confusion
may make the difference between life and death for the
butterflyfish, which makes good its escape in the opposite
direction to that anticipated by the predator.*

LEFT *Slow-moving, the lionfish (Pterois volitans) uses its long
pectoral fins as a driving net to 'shoo' small prey into a tight
corner on the reef. Looking for a way to escape, the prey see what
appears to be a hole in the gauze-like folds of the fins. It is a trap –
a transparent window leading directly to the Lionfish's mouth.*

*Quite different in colour from the rest of its body, the Pacific skink's (*Leiolopisma laterimaculata*) blue tail diverts the attention of predatory birds away from its head. When the bird seizes the tail, it breaks off, allowing the skink to scuttle to safety.*

LEFT *Surprise is usually a good deterrent, and this caterpillar's strategy is especially effective as few predators willingly tangle with a viper. The snake-like eyes on the caterpillar's head have been refined by evolution over countless generations.*

Many beetles store unpleasant-tasting chemicals in their bodies for defensive purposes. They are generally derived from excretory products of the digestion. However, it is not enough simply to be obnoxious – the bug must advertize the fact if it is to avoid predators. This Palm beetle of the Alunus species uses a typical 'warning' pattern of yellow and black which is understood by birds to signal an unpleasant experience.

A characteristic of bugs belonging to the Hemiptera order, like these firebugs (Pyrrhocoris apterus)*, is their ability to produce poisons so toxic that they kill other insects such as ants on contact. Unfortunately, the poison – which eats through the cuticle layer of their enemy's exoskeleton – is so powerful that it is dangerous to the Firebugs themselves. The bright warning coloration means that they seldom have to use it.*

Like most of the creatures of the sea, the Killer whale (Orca orca) is marked with a dark back so it is invisible from above, whilst a pale belly acts as camouflage against the underside of the water's surface. The camouflage is useful for hunting, but the distinctive markings also serve a social purpose with the family group.

RIGHT *Skunks (Mephitis mephitis) can spray a fine, foul-smelling liquid to drive their enemies away, but this is a last resort. They always give good warning, stamping their feet and displaying their distinctive coat markings by raising the tail and walking stiff-legged.*

Hard to distinguish from a real wasp, the hoverfly (Chrysotoxum cautum) visits flowers just like the insect it mimics. There are more than 4,600 species of hoverflies, and most of them borrow the warning coloration of 'armed' insects as a defence.

LEFT *Genuine wasps carry a poison containing a cocktail of chemicals designed to cause maximum pain and shock. Common wasps (Vespula vulgaris) usually feed on nectar and sweet plant juices, saving the sting as a defence. Once stung, predators tend to avoid yellow and black insects for ever.*

*The Arrow poison frog from Costa Rica carries a powerful poison
that acts on the central nervous system. Used by Colombian
Indians to annoint their arrowheads, brightly coloured little frogs
of the Dendrobates family are abundant in the rainforest, where
their vivid colours warn birds and snakes 'Don't touch!'*

*The highly venomous Coral snake (Micrurus nigrocinctus) is
secure in the knowledge that its distinctive red and black markings
are such common warning colours in the animal kingdom that few
predators will dare to attack. Most warning coloration tactics rely
on predatory animals learning by experience which colours are
associated with unpleasant stings, bites or tastes. The Coral snake
poses a problem. As its assailants invariably die, it means that
predatory species cannot learn of the Coral snake's dangerous
nature by experience.*

INDEX